D1195872

TEEN LIFE™

FREQUENTLY ASKED QUESTIONS ABOUT

Being Gifted

Tracie
O'Connor

ROSEN
PUBLISHING®

New York

Published in 2008 by The Rosen Publishing Group, Inc.
29 East 21st Street, New York, NY 10010

First Edition

Library of Congress Cataloging-in-Publication Data

O'Connor, Frances.
Frequently asked questions about being gifted / Frances O'Connor.
    p. cm.—(FAQ: teen life)
Includes bibliographical references and index.
ISBN-13: 978-1-4042-1938-0
ISBN-10: 1-4042-1938-2
1. Gifted teenagers. 2. Adolescent psychology. I. Title.

BF724.3.G53O36 2007
155.5087'9—dc22

                                            2007000381

Manufactured in the United States of America

Introduction

Being gifted is exactly as it sounds: a person who is gifted has exceptional talents that set her apart from other students her age. That person's gifts are usually measured by intelligence quotient (IQ) tests, achievement tests, and teacher evaluations. As you can probably guess, the gifted person, as with any human being, is much more than what is said about her on paper. Gifted people use their unique combination of natural abilities and the ability to pick up new skills very rapidly to be successful in academics and the real world.

If you are gifted and reading this, you will find ways to see your life and your incredible capacity to learn from many angles, and you will understand more about your development. If a friend or family member is gifted, then you will find out how this person sees the world and what types of skills she has.

How Is Being Gifted Determined?

The standard way of determining someone's gifted status is by measuring IQ. In 1905, French psychologists Alfred Binet and Theodore Simon created a test to measure students' abilities. Their test was actually designed to look at students who most likely wouldn't perform well in a regular school

For many years, Binet and Simon's IQ test has been the authority and standard for measuring intelligence.

and would need a nonstandard type of education. Only by chance did it also measure students whose intelligence was on the high end of the spectrum. Later, psychologist Lewis Terman published Binet and Simon's test in America and refined it to compare mental age with chronological age. This result became known as the intelligence quotient, or IQ. When a student takes an IQ test and it's determined that he or she has an IQ above the average of 100, it means that this person has a great potential to do well in academics.

Being gifted isn't only determined by IQ. In fact, it's unjust to measure all students just by their IQs when it has been proven that people can be talented in ways that far exceed the range in which they're tested. Other ways that being gifted can be measured are specific academic aptitude (talent in a subject such as math or science), one's creativity (talent at sculpture, poetry, or writing music), leadership, and visual and performing arts skills.

There is an array of definitions of being gifted, from the conservative, IQ-based to more personal profiles of students' capabilities. The following are a few organizations' guidelines and definitions of giftedness:

The U.S. Department of Education

This is how the federal government defines gifted young people: "Students, children, or youth who give evidence of high achievement capability in areas such as intellectual, creative, artistic, or leadership capacity, or in specific academic fields, and who need services and activities not ordinarily provided by the school in order to fully develop those capabilities."

The Jacob K. Javits Gifted and Talented Students Education Program

This program provides grants for education programs serving bright children from low-income families. It gives this definition of gifted: "The term gifted and talented student means children and youths who give evidence of higher performance capability in such areas as intellectual, creative, artistic, or leadership capacity, or in specific academic fields, and who require services or activities not ordinarily provided by the schools in order to develop such capabilities fully."

The National Association for Gifted Children

This organization defines a gifted person as follows: "Someone who shows, or has the potential for showing, an exceptional level of performance in one or more areas of expression. Some of these abilities are very general and can affect a broad spectrum of the person's life such as leadership skills or the ability to think creatively. Some are very specific talents and are only evident in particular circumstances such as a special aptitude in mathematics, science, or music. The term giftedness provides a general reference to this spectrum of abilities without being specific or dependent on a single measure or index. It is generally recognized that approximately 5 percent of the student population, or three million children, in the United States are considered gifted."

Cultural Biases

Being gifted is largely a Western concept. Not all cultures and ethnicities believe that intelligence can be measured. Even though you may be gifted according to various standards, you may be part of a culture that does not believe that a person needs to be named as such. This does not mean that people don't recognize your talents. They most likely do, but they may not feel that it's important for you to have a gifted designation.

How Do I Know If I'm Gifted?

If you're gifted, you probably already know, as most assessments take place in elementary school. Also, if you're in a class or school that's labeled "gifted and talented," this is a tip-off. It's considered pretty controversial for parents and psychologists to reveal actual IQs to students (to avoid placing undue pressure on kids), but you may find yourself in a class situation in which the teacher asks you to self-evaluate (describe your own learning speed and abilities) and join groups that are appropriate to your level.

If you are not gifted, it doesn't mean that you are not smart or talented. You might be an amazing artist, a skilled athlete, or a talented musician. Or you might just be an interesting person who doesn't have a particular academic focus. Gifted people are in the minority, and if you find out that you are not gifted, take comfort that there are many people just like you. Also, there are gifted students who haven't been tested and named gifted. These young people may feel that school is unchallenging and they may be bored, which results in their not putting effort into their work. This reaction reduces the likelihood that teachers will test them for giftedness.

Get Tested

If you think you're gifted because classes are not challenging, or you find that you pick up skills very quickly, urge your parents to ask the teacher to test you. (School administrators must get your guardian's permission before they are allowed to test you.) Approach your parents about the experiences you're having in school, that the work is too easy and the projects less than challenging. Because gifted capabilities are usually tested and confirmed in elementary school, it might come as a surprise to

Being a gifted person, you may find yourself bored in a class of attentive students. If you feel that the school is not challenging, look into taking higher-level subjects.

your family or teacher that you want to be tested now. Keep your cool if this frustrates you, and present your position calmly and firmly to the authority figures in your life. Your cause will be taken seriously, and they might be surprised to see your mature self-awareness.

You might be struggling under the weight of a gift that, up until now, has felt like a burden. Gifted children who are undiagnosed feel as if they've been burdened with an additional sight or knowledge of a subject or situation that no one else their age can see. Knowing more about a subject indicates that you have a natural ability to do well, and you can accept the type of challenge that will make you grow. A difficult part of your school life might have been that your special gifts had gone unnoticed so far. Perhaps you were in crowded classes where a teacher couldn't see your abilities, or the opportunity never presented itself for you to shine. If you're confident that you have a gift, talk to your parents and teacher about being tested by a school psychologist or learning specialist for gifted abilities.

What Does Being Gifted and Talented Entail?

Gifted students have high IQs and the ability to grow in academic and creative ways very quickly. This means they work differently from their peers to challenge themselves as they grow.

In other words, giftedness has to do with how you score on standardized tests, and it means doing something about your gifts. That usually means finding a learning environment and approach that keep your interest and work for you. You might be placed in the environment during your regular school day, or it could be supplemental to your school. Whether in school or in addition to school, it will provide you with the right kind of "food for thought."

Educators use different strategies to teach gifted students. If you are gifted, you might find yourself in one of the following scenarios to hone your talents:

➤ You might be allowed to take part in learning experiences not included in standard courses, either outside the classroom or during class time. For example, a teacher might modify the curriculum or instruction so that the content or pace at which he teaches is suitable to you. Or a teacher might mix up the way in which he usually teaches the subject to go faster than he would with average students, or he may change the number of steps required for you to perform. For example, a teacher may change a science experiment to include more steps and more results for you to record.

➤ You might be given extra projects for outside the classroom that are related to the subject being studied at school. For example, an English assignment might be to interview town officials.

➤ You might be grouped with other students to receive appropriately challenging instruction. Ability, size, and interests could determine which groups you're placed in. The teacher might place students in groups that study the subject together according to their skill levels and interests.

Over time, educators have developed teaching strategies that work best for gifted learners, and they have begun to apply them in regular classrooms as well as in classes that are for gifted students. They have discovered that gifted students do well in settings that work to challenge them in positive ways. Being gifted requires being ready to think in unconventional ways that are sometimes described as thinking "outside the box." If you're a gifted student, you should go to school prepared to work in unusual ways to sharpen your skills. Being gifted entails being ready to do the work to keep the finely tuned engines of your brain running while understanding which methods work best for you.

one

WHAT ARE MY CHALLENGES?

Being gifted comes with pressures that other students may not face. If you are gifted, your friends, classmates, teachers, and maybe your parents might expect you to be "on" all the time, meaning that you must always perform well and grasp new concepts easily.

Academic Pressures

You already know that being gifted means that you have special abilities, but like anyone else, you will be better at some tasks than others. This pressure can feel enormous in the face of homework assignments, activities, projects, tests, and then college admission exams. Luckily, there are places to go for help when the pressure mounts. There are Web sites that can help with any feelings of depression and

Being gifted doesn't necessarily mean that school will be easy for you. Many young people grow depressed as a result of academic pressures.

inadequacy you might have as a result of school pressures. Two sites you might find helpful are www.depressedteens.com and www.sengifted.org.

Intentional Underachievement

Surprisingly, you might respond to outside pressures to be perfect or pressures from within to achieve great things by performing poorly. You're not alone. A lot of gifted students achieve less than what they know they can do. Why are gifted students sometimes underachievers? If you are a gifted student, you might be familiar with the frustration that comes with waiting for the class to catch up to where you are, or the frustration of not getting picked to answer questions because your teacher assumes you have the right answers and picks someone else. These are just two of the reasons why students who are gifted tend to underperform. Another might be that it's simply too much pressure to operate constantly at the level at which others expect.

If you are a gifted student and you notice that this is your pattern, it's a pitfall to which you should pay attention. You are probably not in the correct learning environment. You might be in a pretty good one by your city's standards but not the ideal environment for you. You will have to ask yourself if your needs are being met. Take your own temperature on this issue. Do you feel frustrated that you're far ahead of the rest of your class? Do you feel your teacher ignores you because he or she doesn't have time to give you the advanced work that might keep you from getting bored? Do you feel the heat of the spotlight from parents and teachers and would rather stay out of the blinding

Myths and Facts
About Being Gifted

Teachers love gifted kids. Fact: ➡ Some teachers are fantastic at teaching gifted students. Others, surprisingly, are not and might be prejudiced against them. Some teachers really enjoy the challenge of teaching students who like taking on different types of projects and who grasp concepts quickly. Others may feel prepared to teach only the average learner and are uncomfortable engaging a gifted student.

For gifted students, school is a piece of cake. Fact ➡ Gifted students don't necessarily find every subject easy. Being gifted means that someone has the ability to achieve academic success, but she's not Superwoman. When gifted students first encounter a new subject, they have to acquire skills and understanding just as everyone else does. Gifted students may pick up certain skills faster than others, but they are not going to be perfect at every subject all the time.

Listening to classical music as a baby is what makes people gifted. Fact While studies have indicated that listening to classical music can increase a child's aptitude, humans must constantly be in a good learning environment in order to grow. When gifted is defined by a high IQ, it is most likely a result of a combination of genetic traits and being put in a successful learning environment. Classical music isn't the only thing that will make a person gifted at birth or in early childhood.

 Gifted students love school. Fact Some studies estimate that 20 percent of high school dropouts are gifted. This suggests that most high schools, which are geared toward the average learner, do not work for the gifted learner. Many gifted dropouts find that the traditional learning environment and its teaching methods are dissatisfying and a waste of brainpower.

 If you are gifted, you will never be cool. Fact Unlike the nerd in the movies whose glasses are taped in the middle, and for whom gym class is a misery of basketballs hitting him in the head, life for gifted students is not that way. Gifted students, like any other middle and high school students, come in a variety of shapes and sizes, and are not destined any more than anyone else to be unpopular.

glare? If you answer yes to these questions, it's a problem with a fairly easy solution. Have a conversation with a teacher you trust or your parents and tell them that you feel what's happening in class is not right for you and that you'd like to work in a different way. Teachers can be your allies. Creative teachers can come up with a learning plan that fits your needs. This plan should resolve some of the negative feelings you're having.

If you feel that even though assignments are not challenging, but nonetheless difficult to complete, you might want to track your behavior. Just because somebody has a high IQ does not mean that he or she is immune to learning disabilities or the ability to concentrate, which is a sign of attention deficit disorder (ADD) or attention deficit/hyperactivity disorder (ADHD). If you think that work is tough for you because it's difficult to concentrate, talk to an adult, be it a family member, counselor, or teacher.

Desire for Perfection

If you are gifted, you may have a different set of social and emotional needs than other students. Gifted students are more likely to be perfectionists. You are used to performing well and might be hard on yourself to perform well all the time. This desire to be perfect and the ability to envision a more perfect world frequently lead gifted students to be politically aware and involved in environmental and social justice causes, like preserving rain forests and helping their city's homeless population. If you are gifted and feel this heightened desire to change the world, you can have the expectation that others in your community feel

Many gifted students like to excel outside of school as well, such as by joining organizations that support social causes.

equally passionate. It can be disappointing when your peers don't show the same level of enthusiasm or even a basic awareness about the same issues. It's important to recognize these feelings of disappointment and talk about how they make you feel. In talking about these feelings, you will feel less alone and can find friends who share your same goals.

two

WHY DO I CONSTANTLY EXPERIENCE ACADEMIC ANXIETY?

Being gifted often involves superior academic talents. However, even though you may excel academically, you are not necessarily free from academic anxiety, which can strike us all on the day of the test or the night before that report is due. Whether you are experiencing mild or severe academic anxiety, you will have some inward and outward signs of worry. These symptoms are a result of the biochemical changes that take place in the fight-or-flight response and are a means of the body holding up a red flag to notify you that it's having trouble dealing with a set of influences. These signs and symptoms can be hardly noticeable to the person experiencing them though really obvious to everyone in the room.

Symptoms of Mild Academic Anxiety

- Dizziness
- Nausea or stomachache
- Sweaty, clammy palms
- Red blotches on the face
- Blushing
- Headache
- A rise in pitch of speaking voice
- Negative thoughts about failing the assignment or running out of time
- Self-doubt about abilities in the subject area
- Fear of embarrassment in front of classmates, friends, and the teacher
- Fear of failure

Symptoms of Severe Academic Anxiety

- Numbness in hands and feet
- Hypochondria (fear of getting sick)
- Inability to sleep
- Severe dizziness or loss of consciousness
- Difficulty breathing and feelings of being choked
- Paranoid thoughts of being judged by people or disliked immediately
- Obsessive, repetitive thoughts that are hard to stop
- Fear of embarrassment in front of classmates, friends, and the teacher

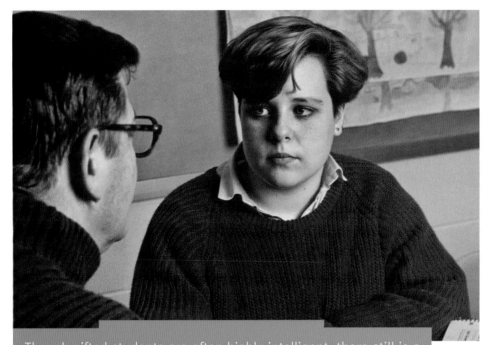

Though gifted students are often highly intelligent, there still is a lot to be learned from talking to professionals such as guidance counselors.

➡ Fear of feeling anxiety
➡ Depression
➡ Sadness and feeling weighed down by heavy worry
➡ Unending panic and upset that doesn't seem to be related to any one particular event

If you are convinced that your academic anxiety is off the charts, it's important to remember that it's common for everyone to experience some worries about school—worry or concern is a healthy emotion in small doses. The best way to determine if you are experiencing regular levels of anxiety about school is by talking to your school psychologist, social worker, or guidance counselor. He or she can ask you some questions about the types of anxiety you've been experiencing and can help you work out strategies for managing this anxiety. He or she can also help you sort out your own thoughts more clearly by repeating some of your statements back to you. This outside person is really helpful in identifying the degree to which pressures are at work in your life simply because he or she is not as close to your emotions as you are. This person is also the key link to maintaining wellness. He or she can recommend exercises to keep you feeling in control of this powerful anxiety that can otherwise make you feel as if you're drowning.

The "Trickle Down" Effects of Academic Anxiety

There are obvious connections between a person's thoughts and emotions and the effects they have on the body. There are also less obvious ways that academic anxiety can wear a person down when left untreated. Bodies rely on pretty complicated networks of emotions and thoughts. In the same way minds and emotions are connected to how bodies feel, emotions and fears about academics are linked to emotions about other areas of life. Like an overflowing faucet, academic anxiety can trickle out of the sink of school situations and down into other layers of emotions, where people store feelings about self-image, ability to have healthy friendships, appearance, and self-esteem.

When academic anxiety affects your physical and emotional health, such as your eating and socializing habits, it may be time to talk to a professional.

Academic anxiety can also cause you to bring negative feelings to regular interactions you have with friends and family and cause these experiences to sour. You may start worrying about something a friend has said when joking around, or you might feel bad about a pointer your coach gives you after school. You might even take a parent's concerned comment to mean that he or she is angry with you. This is the academic anxiety doing the talking, or feeling, for you. Simply put, you are still wearing the emotional glasses of academic anxiety and will see other life situations through these lenses of worry and defeat.

Academic anxiety can also trickle down into daily habits, such as eating. Where you may never have had a problem eating your three square meals a day with some healthy snacks thrown in, academic anxiety can cause you to be an emotional eater who relies on food for comfort. It is not that you have suddenly developed a poor eating habit out of nowhere. It's academic anxiety at your emotional center that is reaching its tentacles out and grabbing at your other emotions, twisting them into knotted negative feelings. Or you may be neglecting eating due to stress and other obligations.

Academic anxiety that's gone out of control can make you develop less than charming social habits—such as talking abruptly, interrupting others to talk about your own situation, or being absentminded about friends' birthdays and special events. Because you are feeling so worried about your performance in school, academic anxiety can make you experience major mood swings. Minor happenings such as the bus being late can make you feel as if your head is going to explode.

The good news about the symptoms of academic anxiety is that as soon as you identify what is affecting you, you have solved half of this complicated puzzle. Once you recognize that your anxiety isn't necessarily about the situation you're in, but rather the powerful academic anxiety that's crowding its way to your thoughts from other life situations, the better off you are. You can take this self-awareness to that counselor, psychologist, or social worker and begin to work on ways to put academic anxiety into a much smaller place in your thoughts.

Social Pressures

Along with the different set of emotional needs that may make you a perfectionist, you will have different experiences from your peers as well. Remember that these experiences are not worse than what everyone else is experiencing in school, but simply different. It may feel weird to be the only one who is reaching to answer a teacher's questions or who gets excited about science lab, but it doesn't make you a teacher's pet. It makes you someone who likes science. If you have classmates who are interested in labeling you for your likes, ignore them. What makes people interesting and well liked as adults is that they are interested. What makes you unusual now will make you a hit later in life. Liking subjects that are highly exploratory, such as mapmaking or how zero gravity happens in space, might not be the theme of every conversation at lunch, but it doesn't mean you shouldn't talk about such fascinating subjects.

School is a stepping stone to the real world outside of school, where scientists, astronauts, geologists, professors, and countless

Being gifted doesn't mean that you can't have friends who have other interests and talents than you do. Good friendships are about sharing your differences.

other professionals ponder equations, write complicated music, and make decisions you are considering now at your young age. When you arrive in the postschool world, people are more likely to hear your thoughts and will be impressed by your ability to think of creative ways to solve problems.

It's not impossible to find friends who are on the same page. Some students are afraid to show their giftedness for fear of being called nerds. Sometimes all it takes to make friends with someone who is gifted like you is to make someone feel comfortable. Let that person you like know that in the high school world of "I don't care," it's OK to talk about "smart" things—you like those topics, too. If you think you're gifted, that is, if you have experiences of wanting to move faster than the pace your class is moving, or you find yourself doing very well, chances are you do have a special aptitude, or gift. Talk to your classmates who are also doing well in the subject. They may become your friends. Whatever you do, don't hide your gifts. They are what make you unique, and they are your fire. You were blessed with a strong mind, and this has a special meaning, even if you can't see its purpose yet. The world is a big, wonderful place. By applying your gifts, you will bring a great light as you travel through life's adventures.

three

ARE ALL GIFTED PEOPLE LONELY?

Gifted teens often feel lonely and/or depressed because they feel left out of the crowd or different. Loneliness is a perfectly natural part of the maturation process for everyone. Loneliness can often lead to depression, and loneliness can be a symptom of depression. Lonely people, though, are not necessarily depressed, and the conditions can be easily confused.

Depression manifests itself as withdrawal, anxiety, lack of motivation, and sadness. All of these symptoms closely mirror loneliness. While loneliness can usually be treated through counseling or various self-help strategies and techniques, depression often requires more intensive therapy and/or medication, depending on the depth and severity of the problem. It's important to understand how loneliness and depression differ.

10 FACTS ABOUT BEING GIFTED

1 Three million children in the United States are considered gifted.

2 Studies have found that 20 percent of high school dropouts are gifted.

3 Albert Einstein, a gifted scientist, was thought to be unintelligent when he was in grammar school. His teacher told his parents there wasn't much hope for him.

4 In 1901, the first school for gifted children opened in Worcester, Massachusetts.

5 There are more than 50,000 members in the American chapter of Mensa.

6 Only twenty-eight states have mandates to provide services for gifted students, according to a 2005 report from the National Association for Gifted Children and the Council of State Directors for the Gifted.

7 When a student takes an IQ test and it's determined that he or she has an IQ above the average of 100, it means that this person has a great potential to do well in academics.

8 With an IQ of 228, Marilyn vos Savant has the highest reported intelligence quotient in the world. She is in the *Guinness Book of World Records* and writes a weekly "Ask Marilyn" column for *Parade* magazine.

9 Geena Davis, who costarred in the movie *Thelma and Louise*, is a member of Mensa and has an IQ in the genius range.

10 Most experts believe that people are born gifted.

How Loneliness and Depression Differ

The most noticeable difference between loneliness and depression may be the way in which the sufferer reacts to the condition. Dr. Robert Weiss, a sociologist at the University of Massachusetts, compares the two typical reactions: "In loneliness, there is a drive to rid oneself of one's distress . . . In depression, there is instead a surrender to it." Studies have shown that lonely and depressed people feel hopeless in equal numbers, and both groups are susceptible to suicidal thoughts and aggressive behavior. On the other hand, feelings of shame and guilt are more closely associated with depression. A 1979 study showed that depression, unlike loneliness, was categorized by anger

Loneliness is common among gifted people, as many feel that they have little in common with others.

and dissatisfaction with nonsocial aspects of a person's life. Loneliness, however, was characterized by a low occurrence of social interaction, while depressed people were less reluctant to join social gatherings.

Depression is also something that can be more common and pronounced in certain seasons, occurring most often during the winter months. Loneliness, on the other hand, tends to be a more constant state. Nevertheless, people can function in a depressed state for an extended time. If the condition persists and even gets worse, then medical help is called for. This is what is then

Depression, along with loneliness, often strikes gifted people. There is hope, however, and those experiencing these feelings should seek professional help.

called clinical depression, indicating that the person's ability to function in society has been strongly affected.

A study conducted using the University of California–Los Angeles (UCLA) Loneliness Scale, the Belcher Extended Loneliness Scale (BELS), the Beck Depression Inventory, and patient questionnaires about social and emotional loneliness helped further delineate the differences between depression and loneliness. The main differences between the two conditions were broken down into four main categories. The first was the relative focus and scope of one's dissatisfaction. Lonely people tend to be dissatisfied with interpersonal issues, whereas depressed people are more often unhappy with matters on a more global scale. Second, the duration of the patient's feelings can help distinguish loneliness from depression. The longer the feeling has been in place, the greater the likelihood the condition is depression. The third distinguishing characteristic would be the feeling of guilt, which is more often associated with depression than loneliness. Finally, depressed people tend to develop more secondary disorders than lonely people do, including eating disorders (generally overeating or undereating), sleep disorders (such as insomnia), and alcohol abuse.

Someone who suspects he or she is suffering from either loneliness or depression or perhaps both should immediately seek help from friends and family and seriously consider going to see a therapist. Left untreated, loneliness can turn into depression and can result in a wide range of self-destructive and potentially dangerous behaviors. Don't hesitate to seek and accept help. Let people guide you out of the loneliness within which you feel isolated and trapped. Should you be a friend helping a lonely or depressed person who does not seem to be improving, encourage that person strongly to get professional help.

four

WHAT SHOULD I DO WITH MY TALENTS?

Being gifted has many high points. As a member of this group, you can learn faster, and more wholly, about the world and grow in your natural aptitude to a level most of your classmates will achieve only when they are much older. Being gifted also means that you're in good company. You are among the ranks of those who have been responsible for the most important scientific discoveries, meaningful mechanical inventions, inspiring leadership of movements, and breathtaking artistic expressions of our time. You have the same capacity for wonder and accomplishment as Marie Curie, Isaac Newton, the Wright brothers, Gandhi, Henri Matisse, Georgia O'Keeffe, Michelangelo, Beethoven, and Bob Dylan, to name a few.

According to the Mensa *Gifted Children's Handbook*, a gifted person has some fantastic, unique characteristics:

Bill Gates *(right)*, founder of Microsoft and richest man in the world, has used his intelligence to revolutionize computing and philanthropy.

- Shows quick mastery and recall of factual information
- Usually sees more or gets more out of a story, film, etc., than others
- Has an unusually advanced vocabulary for age or grade level
- Needs little external motivation to follow through in work that initially excited him or her
- Strives for perfection; not easily satisfied with his or her speed and products
- Adapts readily to new situations
- Can express himself or herself well
- Displays a keen sense of humor
- Shows emotional sensitivity
- Is sensitive to beauty
- Is a high–risk taker; is adventurous and speculative
- Has a sense of justice and fairness

Changing the World

These are all positive characteristics that, when added to the genetic and social formula that is uniquely yours, is a mixture for success. Because you have been able to do things with relative ease, you might also have high aspirations. Many gifted people are able to envision a world in which they can create an impact. They oftentimes use their talents and vision to enact change. Many become leaders of movements, whether it's creating a new style of painting, inventing a lifesaving medical device, or becoming a leader of a political cause. With the guidance of great teachers, mentors, and parents, you can harness your intelligence to power new ideas and change the

Gifts, such as intelligence, are rare and should be taken advantage of to their fullest potentials. Teaching and leading others is a great way to make the most of your talents.

shape of the world. Imagine that—gifts to change the world with your thoughts and actions.

Many gifted young people ask what they should do now that they know they are gifted. Two words: use it! Don't let anyone get in the way of you growing into the best version of yourself. Your talent— regardless of whether it's creative, scientific, mathematic, or of a leadership kind—is special. It should be exercised whenever, and however, possible. The challenge that many gifted students face is going to school in a system that is designed to meet the needs of the average learner. At best, the regular school system will meet most gifted students' needs, but most likely, regular classes will not take care of all needs.

Turn to Your Teacher

Teachers are your allies, but not all teachers have the time and resources to teach gifted students. If you are a gifted student

Teachers can help you make the most of your gifts. They can expose you to the various opportunities available to you as a talented person.

who feels you are in the wrong environment, it doesn't mean this can't change with the aid of the right teacher. The right teacher will help you come up with a plan that best meets your needs and, if necessary, recommend a separate class or program that might provide a more challenging learning environment. Even if you are a gifted student in the right environment, there are always elements or parts of your educational plan that you can work on with your teacher to make your experience more fulfilling. In the right environment, it's still your responsibility to be self-aware about your progress and to discuss with your teacher the best type of learning for your abilities.

Take Charge of Your Learning

First, know yourself. As a gifted student, once you learn that you are responsible for your own knowledge and the path you will take to gain the most knowledge, you will feel great about yourself. It may sound stressful to think about being responsible for your own education, but being responsible in this case means that you can blaze your own path to the information you yearn for once you understand your own aptitudes (natural abilities) and inclinations (likes).

Understanding that part of responsibility shouldn't be stressful, but rather freeing. Think about your own learning style and the way you process information. Do you like to read an explanation first, and then dive into the hands-on part? Or do you prefer to experiment first and read the explanation later? Do you prefer to work in a group to brainstorm ideas, or do you prefer to work alone to think about various solutions you'll later present to the group? Make a mental note of what works best for you, and carry this with you into each learning situation.

Know Your Options

Additional educational approaches that might work for you are explained below. Read each and ask yourself if this is a way you should be working in the classroom to increase your abilities:

➤ **Independent study.** In this type of learning, you manage your learning through projects of your own choosing and design. The teacher acts as a guide and not as the person who creates your assignments.

- **Cooperative learning.** This instructional method allows you to work in small groups in class, with each student in a group taking on a specific role or task.
- **Portfolio assessment.** In this type of approach, you make a portfolio of the work you do, and your teacher assesses the progress of your work at a set time, like at the end of the term or school year.
- **Talent development.** You enroll in specifically designed programs, like a math-centered program, which focus directly on improving your talents.
- **Dual enrollment.** You would take college classes in addition to attending high school to increase your academic challenges.

Meet Like Minds

Even if you are around gifted students at school, it can help to join clubs or groups to work on your skills. People who have gifts in the same areas as you—whether it's science, math, writing, leadership, or the fine arts—can make wonderful friends. In the company of your peers who share the same aptitudes and activity choices, you can really soar by encouraging each other to reach greater heights of creativity and skill building. This is not to mention the fun you can have in feeling at home among people who read the same books and play the same games as you do.

Mensa is an organization for people whose intelligence quotients qualify them for membership. American Mensa (www.us.mensa.org) has a committee devoted to children and

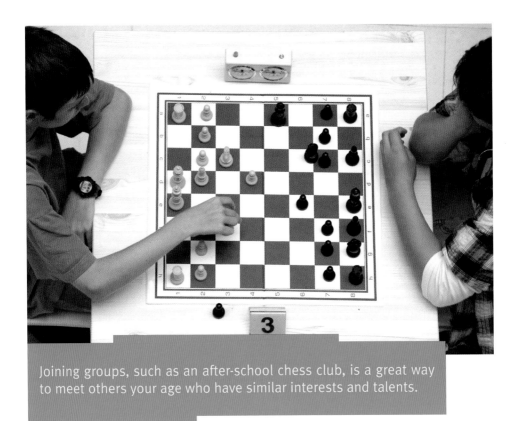

Joining groups, such as an after-school chess club, is a great way to meet others your age who have similar interests and talents.

teenagers who are eligible. American Mensa sponsors events such as a weekend of playing games like Trivial Pursuit and has lists of resources, books, and games. It also hosts links to schools that have gifted classes and has a section devoted to scholarships and grants you can receive as a gifted student.

Find out about other groups for gifted students available in your state and region. Don't be afraid to ask your teachers about clubs at neighboring schools or schools that are a level up from yours. Ask about clubs at a local community college or university. This can be a great way to get "plugged in" to another academic scene that might be a great fit for you.

Reflect on Your Accomplishments

Think about your goals for enjoying your work and becoming further aware of the progress you make in school. Your school-work may seem like an unending chain of events, but think about how good it feels to learn how to do something you didn't know how to do until a short while ago. Think about how good it feels to learn how to ride a bike, knit, or drive a car. It's an awesome new independence and understanding of yourself. Be prepared to set goals every month or two that allow you to look back at what you've learned, and be proud of yourself for putting the time and effort into sharpening your skills.

HOW SHOULD I COPE WITH MY GIFT?

While being gifted is certainly no curse, it does come with its own set of challenges, especially at this time in your life. In high school, you and your peers are searching for your identities and trying to pin down what values are meaningful. In the growing-up process, teenagers end up being very hard on themselves, their friends, and their classmates. Being gifted comes with social pressures and stereotypes that can wrongly label who you are as an individual.

Dealing with Ridicule and Teasing

If you are gifted and are being teased, it stinks. Everyone gets teased for something—for having red hair, for being tall, for being short, for having a big chest, for having a small chest. The list goes on. This doesn't mean that

Though teasing may hurt, it's important to remember that people may treat you badly only because they feel threatened by your advantage over them.

others' teasing defines who you are as a person. Teasing doesn't speak to the truth of who you are. This doesn't mean that it doesn't sting. Teasing has a way of making you wish you didn't have any of the characteristics others notice about you. Ridicule about being gifted can be severe enough to make you wish you weren't gifted.

Why Do People Put You Down?

Think about the reasons why classmates might choose teasing as a means of expressing their thoughts. Your peers are most likely jealous that it takes you a shorter amount of time to arrive at answers that may take them days or weeks to grasp. They also might be jealous of getting less attention and encouragement from their parents and teachers, and less encouragement to learn new things. Your peers might be jealous about how you have piled up so many accomplishments and interests.

Remember that sarcasm is the way many high schoolers express themselves. Maybe some of what you're hearing from classmates is a begrudging admiration for what you're capable of, even though it sounds like a putdown. Sometimes people are less than able at expressing themselves, and their thoughts come out harsher than the way they intend. Last, but not least, some people tease simply because they disagree with you or because they're not capable of maturity and kindness at this point in their lives.

Your Reaction

Think of whether or not you will choose to accept others' opinions of who you are. You do have a choice. You are always more than the terms people come up with to describe you. If classmates call you names, shrug it off. They are most likely just jealous of your test score or the attention you got from the teacher. Their remarks say more about how they feel about themselves than what they're thinking about you. They might be unhappy with their own performance. Shrugging it off is a strategy that works for this reason: your lack of reaction doesn't allow the people teasing you to have any power over you. It makes the people who are doing the teasing feel silly when they think their comment

There are all different types of friends. The best ones, though, respect you for who you are and genuinely enjoy being around you.

hasn't affected you. Their remark was intended to hurt your feelings, and when you don't give them the reaction they were hoping for, they have nowhere to go in the conversation. It stops right there.

If teasing comes as a surprise from someone you like and respect such as a friend, ask why she made the comment. It might be that you're putting your friend down or making her feel inferior without knowing it. Perhaps you've accidentally hurt her feelings by teasing her about a lower grade, or maybe you have been bragging a bit too much about accomplishments. Your friends need you to support them as they work on improving their skills, too.

Choosing Your Friends Wisely

Think about your friends. They're your support system, and they experience many of the same things you do. This can make you feel closer to them than your own family. That's why it's important to choose your friends wisely. Befriend people who will always have your best interests in mind and who will help you make smart decisions. Try to think about the differences between a good friend and a bad friend.

What Makes a Good Friend?

A good friend might tease you, but it's an agreed-upon type of teasing that doesn't go too far. It's the type of teasing that's an admiring kind, like when someone has a crush on you and he or she teases and makes sarcastic jokes, rather than coming out and saying it.

Being best friends isn't always about having fun and laughing all the time. Those who are closest to you are those with whom you can share your deepest feelings.

Your friend is competitive in a good way. This person encourages you to perform better in class by studying with you or offering to quiz you on vocabulary or science and math formulas. This person, if she is gifted, too, doesn't encourage ganging up against non-gifted kids to make you feel like it's "us against them." This isn't healthy—or fair to your classmates.

Good friends don't chip away at your confidence by giving away your secrets or allowing jealousy to turn them into gossips who talk about you. They are people whom you can always talk to, especially when you hit a rough patch.

What Makes a Bad Friend?

You can imagine that a bad friend is someone who is the opposite of these things and for whom your being gifted is a burden, rather than a neat part of who you are. A bad friend is embarrassed by your gifts and doesn't seem to understand why you like to grow as fast as you do. A bad friend is also someone who might look at your giftedness as a quick way to an A. This person might ask you to cheat or do his homework, which might feel great at first but isn't "helping" as much as it is that person using you. Watch out for people who pose as friends and try to flatter you into using your gifts to benefit them. In the end, this type of friend isn't a friend at all. He is a user who is trying to get a free pass to doing well without working hard.

How Can I Deal with Pressure from Family and Teachers?

Our families and teachers—we love and like them, but we can't choose them from a crowd as we do our friends. We have to accept them for who they are, and they should accept us for our gifts and our flaws.

If your parents and teachers are putting pressure on you to perform as only a superhuman or robot can, talk about it. Inform each person that you feel he or she is asking you to operate on overload and that you are trying to manage your time and abilities to perform well within the school day, at

Sitting down and talking with a parent is a great way to communicate your need for a social life while dealing with the pressures of school.

home, in sports, and wherever else you do. Ask your parents or teacher to help you make a plan to balance all of your tasks and still have some free time.

Keeping Yourself in Check

There's a difference between being mentally advanced and being socially and emotionally ahead. Keep in mind that even though you think you understand something, you are still a teenager who is under the guidance of parents and teachers. Those who are in charge of you have the life experience and

Ten Great Questions to Ask When You're Asking for Help

1 Should I have my IQ tested?

2 If I'm gifted, should I worry about performing well on simple tasks if I know I can perform well on bigger ones?

3 Whom can I talk to about joining a talented and gifted program?

4 How do I know when to ask for academic help?

5 Whom do I need to tell that I'm gifted? What should I tell my friends?

6 Can I participate in nonacademic activities?

7 Will my children be gifted?

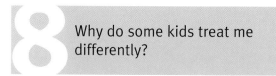

8 Why do some kids treat me differently?

How should I push myself to do better without putting too much pressure on myself?

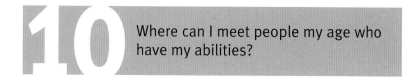

10 Where can I meet people my age who have my abilities?

know-how to make decisions regarding you and know some things that you are incapable of knowing at such a young age.

Living a Complete Life

Gifted teens often feel like their needs aren't being met emotionally. Interactions with peers can be painful reminders that classmates only want to ridicule, while interactions with parents and teachers can lead someone to believe that she should only be thinking about achieving. Some parents deal with their child's giftedness by ignoring it but then praising their child to others. Other parents don't know what to do with giftedness, so they offer no support, no extra activities, no kind questions about school challenges, but brag to friends and neighbors about their child's abilities. In some cases, gifted students find themselves on the receiving end of negative comments and putdowns from

Just because you are gifted doesn't mean that you can't have a well-rounded, normal life. It's important to take advantage of a lot of different opportunities and be happy.

a sibling who can't understand why so much attention gets showered on this kid in the family. If this kid in the family is you, it is a lot of noise to deal with, and not enough messages to quiet the loneliness you probably feel.

You have your own needs and a right to be heard and loved. Try to create the kinds of respect and intimacy (respectful sharing) you want from other people by spending time with each person. Explain your feelings and thoughts, as well as your needs. Sometimes you think that the world can see your pain when in fact it can't—you've done too good a job of being successful and competent, and quiet about your emotions. Be confident that you can change others' perceptions about you and that, in time, you can develop the kinds of relationships that keep you healthy and growing into the well-rounded person you're meant to be.

anxiety A form of nervousness and/or stress, usually brought about by an upcoming event or responsibility such as a test or a due term paper.

aptitude A special ability to build skills very fast in a particular subject area.

curriculum A list of subjects or disciplines that is arranged to be studied in a particular grade of a particular school.

dual enrollment When high school students take both college classes and regular high school classes to increase the challenge of the subject area. This can also refer to middle school students who are taking high school classes for the same reason.

evaluate To take stock of something, often one's own behavioral patterns.

gift In relation to talent, a gift is a unique ability that a person is born with, which usually requires little effort from the person to be performed.

intelligence The ability to learn, reason, and solve problems. Some believe that intelligence is what a person is born with; others say intelligence is developed when people interact with an environment.

intelligence quotient (IQ) A number that represents a person's intelligence.

IQ test A test that determines a person's intelligence quotient.

learning style The way in which an individual most effectively processes information.

perfectionist A person who needs to feel that his or her achievements are perfect but who ironically is often unable to achieve that perfection.

psychologist A doctor who specializes in treating behavioral disorders or disorders of the mind.

underachievement When a student performs at a level that is far below his or her learning potential and ability to perform at a much higher level.

American Mensa

1229 Corporate Drive West

Arlington, TX 76006-6103

(817) 607-0060

Web site: http://www.us.mensa.org

American Mensa is a group comprising people who score at a certain level on a standardized test. Its Web site lists resources for gifted children, organizations for gifted children and their parents, and a list of facts about being gifted.

Council for Exceptional Children (CEC)

1110 North Glebe Road, Suite 300

Arlington, VA 22201

(703) 620-3660

Web site: http://www.cec.sped.org

This organization provides information about schools, classroom learning methods, and facts about gifted students.

National Association for Gifted Children

1707 L Street NW, Suite 550

Washington, DC 20036

(202) 785-4268

Web site: http://www.nagc.org

CEC provides information by and about teachers of gifted students and about educational opportunities for gifted children.

Supporting Emotional Needs of the Gifted (SENG)
P.O. Box 6074
Scottsdale, AZ 85261
(480) 370-2193
Web site: http://www.sengifted.org
  SENG is a nonprofit organization that provides emotional support resources to gifted children and adults.

Web Sites

Due to the changing nature of Internet links, Rosen Publishing has developed an online list of Web sites related to the subject of this book. This site is updated regularly. Please use this link to access the list:

http://www.rosenlinks.com/faq/begi

Armstrong, Thomas, Ph.D. *You're Smarter Than You Think: A Kid's Guide to Multiple Intelligences.* Minneapolis, MN: Free Spirit Publishing, Inc., 2002.

Berger, Sandra L. *College Planning for Gifted Students: Choosing and Getting Into the Right College.* Austin, TX: Prufrock Press, 2006.

Carlson, Richard, Ph.D. *Don't Sweat the Small Stuff for Teens.* New York, NY: Hyperion, 2000.

Delisle, Jim, and Robert A. Schultz. *More Than a Test Score: Teens Talk About Being Gifted, Talented, or Otherwise Extraordinary.* Minneapolis, MN: Free Spirit Publishing, Inc., 2006.

Evangelista, Beth. *Gifted.* New York, NY: Walker Books for Young Readers, 2005.

Friel, John C., Ph.D., and Linda D. Friel, M.A. *The 7 Best Things Smart Teens Do.* Deerfield Beach, FL: HCI Teens, 2000.

McGraw, Jay. *Life Strategies for Teens.* New York, NY: Fireside Press, 2000.

Armstrong, Thomas, Ph.D. *You're Smarter Than You Think: A Kid's Guide to Multiple Intelligences.* Minneapolis, MN: Free Spirit Publishing, Inc., 2002.

Delisle, Jim,. *Gifted Kids Speak Out.* Minneapolis, MN: Free Spirit Publishing, Inc., 1987.

Delisle, Jim, and Judy Galbraith. *When Gifted Kids Don't Have All the Answers.* Minneapolis, MN: Free Spirit Publishing, Inc., 2002.

Delisle, Jim, and Robert A. Schultz. *More Than a Test Score: Teens Talk About Being Gifted, Talented, or Otherwise Extraordinary.* Minneapolis, MN: Free Spirit Publishing, Inc., 2006.

Evangelista, Beth. *Gifted.* New York, NY: Walker Books for Young Readers, 2005.

Galbraith, Judy. *The Gifted Kids' Survival Guide for Ages 11–18.* Minneapolis, MN: Free Spirit Publishing, Inc., 1983.

Galbraith, Judy. *The Gifted Kids' Survival Guide for Ages 10 and Under.* Minneapolis, MN: Free Spirit Publishing, Inc., 1999.

Galbraith, Judy, Jim Delisle, and Pamela Espeland. *The Gifted Kids' Survival Guide: A Teen Handbook.* Minneapolis, MN: Free Spirit Publishing, Inc., 1997.

Index

P

parents/family, pressure from, 50–53
perfection, desire for, 18–19, 26, 37
portfolio assessment, 41

S

Simon, Theodore, 4–5
social pressures, 26–28, 44

T

talent development, 41
teasing/ridicule, dealing with, 44–48
Terman, Lewis, 5

U

underachievement, intentional, 15–18
U.S. Department of Education, 6

Photo Credits

Designer: Evelyn Horovicz; **Editor:** Nicholas Croce
Photo Researcher: Cindy Reiman